PROPHETIC
PRAYER
JOURNAL

LINDA J. KEMP REVIS

authorHOUSE®

AuthorHouse™
1663 Liberty Drive
Bloomington, IN 47403
www.authorhouse.com
Phone: 1 (800) 839-8640

Published by AuthorHouse   03/24/2016

ISBN: 978-1-5049-8466-9 (sc)
ISBN: 978-1-5049-8467-6 (e)

Library of Congress Control Number: 2016904266

Print information available on the last page.

Any people depicted in stock imagery provided by Thinkstock are models,
and such images are being used for illustrative purposes only.
Certain stock imagery © Thinkstock.

This book is printed on acid-free paper.

All scripture quotes are either from the Holy Bible, King James Version; Holy
Bible, New International Version, Copyright © 1873, 1978, 1984 by International
Bible Society, Colorado Springs, Colorado. Used by permission.

Contents

Introduction

Prayer is an important part of the Christian faith. It is an essential component of life for those who believe in God, through Jesus Christ. Therefore, you must take the time to build a good prayer life. You must seek the answers to your issues through prayer. God will answer you when you seek him with your whole heart.

> *But if from there you seek the LORD your God, you will find him if you seek him with all your heart and with all your soul.*
> *Deuteronomy 4:29*

Prayer is how you seek God. This is why building your prayer life is so important. Establishing a habit of praying as you read scripture is a powerful part of a good prayer life. As you do, your faith will be strengthened and your walk with God will become stronger. You will become more grounded in Christ.

*So then, just as you received
Christ Jesus as Lord, continue to
live your lives in him, rooted and
built up in him, strengthened in
the faith as you were taught, and
overflowing with thankfulness.
Colossians 2:6-7*

When you seek God, you must believe that you
will receive whatever you ask him for. God wants to
bless you, no matter what the need or circumstance.
It is God's wholehearted desire that you have the very
best in life and for your life. He is a loving father who
wants to care for his children.

*And without faith it is impossible
to please God, because anyone
who comes to him must believe
that he exists and that he
rewards those who earnestly
seek him. Hebrews 11:6*

God enjoys being your father. He enjoys meeting your needs. He enjoys seeing you advance in life. Through prayer, you can share those needs with him. Through prayer, you can express to God your innermost feelings, desires, and dreams. In return, God will deposit blessings from heaven upon you, other without restraint.

See what great love the Father has lavished on us, that we should be called children of God! And that is what we are! The reason the world does not know us is that it did not know him. 1 John 3:1

This prayer journal was written to help you grow your prayer life. Use it as a tool to help you move closer to God. Let it become your inspiration for a better walk through life knowing that God is by your side. After all, God said he would always be with you. You must believe this each time you pray.

Keep your lives free from the love of money and be content with what you have, because God has said, "Never will I leave you; never will I forsake you." Hebrews 13:5

As you pray with faith, you discover more of who God is. You then become more in love with him. It strengthens the bond between you and God as you meditate on him. This makes you more committed to God. Seeking his will for your life becomes your daily purpose. You gain a new perspective of who God really is. This all happens when you pray.

Who is he, this King of glory? The LORD Almighty- he is the King of glory. Psalm 24:10

I want you to grow your relationship with God. I want your prayer life to become stronger. I want your life to get better. And it can get better as you take the time to earnestly pray.

*You, God, are my God, earnestly
I seek you; I thirst for you, my
whole being longs for you, in a
dry and parched land where
there is no water. Psalm 63:1*

So enjoy the growth in your relationship with
God and Jesus Christ as you work through this prayer
journal. It is my sincere desire that you experience an
anointed change in your life. I pray that the power of
the Holy Spirit will be with you.

Journaling Your Prayers

It is important to focus on the things God is doing in your life. It is also important to gain insights about what God will do in your life. This is possible through prayer. One way to keep track of what God is doing is by journaling your prayers. This prayer journal can help. In time, you will look back on it to see a portion of God's plan for your life. So be diligent in writing down your spiritual experiences as you work through this *Prophetic Prayer Journal.*

Then the LORD replied: "Write down the revelation and make it plain on tablets so that a herald may run with it. Habakkuk 2:2

In this prayer journal, you will find a *Prophetic Prayer* that I have prayed on your behalf. This is followed by a scripture to help you to prepare to pray for your own needs. There is space to write it down and make notes as your prayers are being answered. Use this space to also thank God as you see evidence of him working in your life.

> *See, the former things have taken place, and new things I declare; before they spring into being I announce them to you."*
> *Isaiah 42:9*

There is a *Personal Reflections* section after each prayer. Use this section to record other prayers, hopes, and dreams for your life. This will help you focus on what you want God to do in your life. Periodically review these and ask God to fulfill them.

> *Teach me to do your will, for you are my God; may your good Spirit lead me on level ground.*
> *Psalm 143:10*

The final section is for *Spiritual Revelation*. This is where you read God's word and listen for him to speak to you. Write down the revelations. Later, look back to see how God's word has come true in your life.

These are the things God has revealed to us by his Spirit. The Spirit searches all things, even the deep things of God. 1 Corinthians 2:10

My prophetic prayer for you is that God will bless you beyond measure! I want you to believe it today and live it for life!

If you believe, you will receive whatever you ask for in prayer. Matthew 21:22

The Power of Prayer

So what is prayer? Why is it so important? Prayer is the opportunity to have your voice heard by God. Whether it is a voice of pain or a voice of joy, God will hear it when you pray. God is listening for your voice right now. Call on him! Let God hear your voice today. He will answer.

This is the confidence we have in approaching God: that if we ask anything according to his will, he hears us. 1 John 5:14

The word of God calls us to a position of prayer as a lifestyle, not something we simply do. We do it because it is how we live. That is why the Bible said to pray continually.

Pray continually.1 Thessalonians 5:17

I wrote this prayer journal to help you to have a more consistent prayer life. A consistent prayer life must become part of your daily activities. It has to become part of your spiritual DNA. When it does, it becomes the source of your daily blessings. It also puts you in a position to bless others. This results from your commitment to periods of regular prayer.

This happened to Peter and John in Acts, chapter 3 of the Bible. Their commitment to regular prayer at the temple put them in a position to bring healing to a lame man. Prayer made it happen.

One day Peter and John were going up to the temple at the time of prayer—at three in the afternoon. Now a man who was lame from birth was being carried to the temple gate called Beautiful, where he was put every day to beg from those going into the temple courts. When he saw Peter and John about to enter, he asked them for money. Act 3:1-3

Peter and John knew that their prayer life was worth more than money could buy.

> Then Peter said, "Silver or gold I do not have, but what I do have I give you. In the name of Jesus Christ of Nazareth, walk." Taking him by the right hand, he helped him up, and instantly the man's feet and ankles became strong. He jumped to his feet and began to walk. Then he went with them into the temple courts, walking and jumping, and praising God. Act 3:6-8

The prayer of Peter and John had power! Your prayer has power, too. But you must learn to access it. When you do, you will see the results.

Prayer power is more potent than any other force available to mankind. And when we have been made partakers in Jesus, who gives us victory over sin and death, we gain strength through prayer power. Prayer is our spiritual weapon.

The weapons we fight with are not the weapons of the world. On the contrary, they have divine power to demolish strongholds. 2 Corinthians 10:4

It is my prayer that as you use this prayer journal, write your personal prayers, and reflect upon the prophetic word over your life, that you will be blessed. I pray that this prayer journal leads you into a closer relationship with God through Jesus Christ. Believe God and see the difference it makes through prayer.

Prayer Builds

Testimonies

Prayer works. Make no mistake about it. I am a witness to prayer working. I have experienced prayer working in me and for me. I received God's divine healing from an esophagus hernia after seven years of constant pain. It made sleeping almost unbearable. But one day my salvation came. My relief came because I prayed and continued praying until I was healed! I cried out to God for help and he heard my petition. He freed me from the pain that was in my body.

So I know that prayer works because the pain is no longer in me. Maybe the pain was sent back to the pit of hell. Or maybe it was crushed and scattered to the four winds of the earth. I don't really know where it went. But what I do know is that it left me! Prayer did its job.

So I know that prayer works. It worked for me because of my faith in God's word to seek him for my healing. God said that if I asked, I would receive; so I asked and I was healed.

> *"Ask and it will be given to you; seek and you will find; knock and the door will be opened to you. Matthew 7:7*

That is why I pray and intercede for others. I want others healed from whatever is afflicting them. I do not want them hurting or sick. And since I experienced healing, I want the same for them. I have no doubt that healing, deliverance, and overcoming obstacles are all possible. The opportunity to be set free through the divine power of God is available to all who seek it.

My ordeal led me to pray more and more when I saw others sick or in need. I started to pray when I heard about people with afflictions. I now pray constantly for God to move in the lives of people and meet their needs.

> *And my God will meet all your needs according to the riches of his glory in Christ Jesus. Philippians 4:19*

So I wrote this prayer journal to let you know that you can be healed, delivered, and changed. You can get beyond your circumstance! It doesn't matter how long you have been in your current condition, Christ will set you free!

You can have a rewarding life. You can reach your destiny. You can be happy. You can become the person God wants you to be. Believe it and receive it today!

John 8:36 So if the Son sets you free, you will be free indeed.

Another reason I pray is because God has commanded us to pray. God does not give idle commandments. All of God's commandments have a purpose; prayer has a purpose. The purpose of prayer is to give you access to God's power. God's power will meet your needs.

I also pray because prayer is an effective way of building a loving relationship with God through Jesus Christ. It is critical that you realize that living for God is not about the rules and regulations; that is not the primary reason. It is about the relationship with God that Christ made possible! That relationship is built on prayer.

For this reason I kneel before the Father, from whom every family in heaven and on earth derives its name. I pray that out of his glorious riches he may strengthen you with power through his Spirit in your inner being. Ephesians 3:14-16

Praying the Scriptures

Scripture is a very important part of building a strong prayer life. In New Testament Synagogues and Churches, the scriptures were often read aloud. They read it almost as if they were offering up prayers to God. In doing so, they were actually prophesying what God had done and what God would do.

The scriptures in this prayer journal are designed to help you do the same thing. It is my prayer that you will experience a rich outpour of God's power from heaven as you use it.

Scripture is God talking to you, and in some instances, God talking about you.

All Scripture is God-breathed and is useful for teaching, rebuking, correcting and training in righteousness, so that the servant of God may be thoroughly equipped for every good work. 2 Timothy 3:16-17

Scripture can teach you to pray. In addition, reading scripture gives you the opportunity to engage in a moment by moment conversation with God. When God speaks to you through his word, you get to know that he is real! You actually get to speak to God and hear him speak back to you. In doing so, you realize your prayers are being answered. This encourages you to spend more time with God. So let prayer become your daily habit of having a conversation with God.

Scripture will move you to pray. It will motivate you to declare what God has done, is doing, and will do. Reading scripture helps you to identify with how God confronts your thoughts, feelings, and circumstances. God loves you enough to show you a way out through his word.

No temptation has overtaken you except what is common to mankind. And God is faithful; he will not let you be tempted beyond what you can bear. But when you are tempted, he will also provide a way out so that you can endure it. 1 Corinthians 10:13

God's word will also prompt you to confess your sins and mistakes. It will help you to confront any issue that stands between you and God. After confession, you get an opportunity to walk in a new light before God, one full of hope and promise. Whatever it might be, scripture will help create a stronger prayer life.

If we confess our sins, he is faithful and just and will forgive us our sins and purify us from all unrighteousness. 1 John 1:9

So use scripture in your prayer life. Let God's word help you assess your personal circumstances as you petition God to resolve them. Let your voice about your own longings, wonderings, and situations find support in God's word. In doing so, you will build a better relationship with God that brings results when you pray.

Then they cried out to the Lord in their trouble, and he brought them out of their distress. Psalm 107:28

Prayer No. 1

PROPHETIC PRAYER

*L*ord, I thank you that you hear me when I pray. I know that when I call on you, you will answer me. Lord help me to be faithful to you as you are to me.

Know that the Lord has set apart his faithful servant for himself; the Lord hears when I call to him Psalms 4:3

My prayer for today:

PERSONAL REFLECTIONS

God wants you to have a good life. He will bless you and remove your sickness to help you live it. Worship invites the favor of God to you. Expect to experience him today.

Worship the Lord your God, and his blessing will be on your food and water. I will take away sickness from among you Exodus 23:25

My prayers, hopes, and dreams:

SPIRITUAL REVELATION

Let the following scripture speak to your heart as you meditate on it. Then, write down the things you hear God saying to you. God has a prophetic message for you. Hear it now!

I pray that out of his glorious riches he may strengthen you with power through his Spirit in your inner being, so that Christ may dwell in your hearts through faith. And I pray that you, being rooted and established in love. Ephesians 3:16-17

My spiritual insights and revelations:

Prayer No. 2

PROPHETIC PRAYER

*D*ear Lord, I pray for your will to be done in my life. Thank you for helping me to know your will. Thank you for the blessings that come with obeying you. I am confident that you hear me.

This is the confidence we have in approaching God: that if we ask anything according to his will, he hears us. 1 John 5:14

My prayer for today:

Personal Reflections

The word of God contains insights on to how to live. Listen to what the will of God is for you in your life. It will make you whole.

> *My son, pay attention to what I say; turn your ear to my words. Do not let them out of your sight, keep them within your heart; for they are life to those who find them and health to one's whole body Proverbs 4:20-22*

My prayers, hopes, and dreams:

SPIRITUAL REVELATION

Let the following scripture speak to your heart as you meditate on it. Then, write down the things you hear God saying to you. God has a prophetic message for you. Hear it now!

May the God of hope fill you with all joy and peace as you trust in him, so that you may overflow with hope by the power of the Holy Spirit. Romans 15:13

My spiritual insights and revelations:

Prayer No. 3

PROPHETIC PRAYER

Heavenly Father, I thank you for hearing me in my pain. I believe you will deliver me because you know my voice. You know me when I call. I expect to be delivered from my current situation.

Listen to my words, Lord, consider my lament Hear my cry for help, my King and my God, for to you I pray. In the morning, Lord, you hear my voice; in the morning I lay my requests before you and wait expectantly. Psalms 5:1-3

My prayer for today:

PERSONAL REFLECTIONS

There will be attacks on you, but they will not result in the end of you. God will defend you, his word, his way, and his will.

Whatever they plot against the Lord he will bring to an end; trouble will not come a second time. Nahum 1:9

My prayers, hopes, and dreams:

SPIRITUAL REVELATION

Let the following scripture speak to your heart as you meditate on it. Then, write down the things you hear God saying to you. God has a prophetic message for you. Hear it now!

This is how we know that we live in him and he in us: He has given us of his Spirit. 1 John 4:13

My spiritual insights and revelations:

Prayer No. 4

PROPHETIC PRAYER

Lord, sometimes I become anxious about the things of life. I somethings become frustrated by my situations. Help me to settle my mind and spirit. Lord, help me to be calm and find peace. Be my protector and shield me now.

Do not be anxious about anything, but in every situation, by prayer and petition, with thanksgiving, present your requests to God. And the peace of God, which transcends all understanding, will guard your hearts and your minds in Christ Jesus. Philippians 4:6-7

My prayer for today:

PERSONAL REFLECTIONS

True protection can only come from God. He is the one who will sustain your life in trying times. God will restore your life.

> *The Lord protects and preserves them—they are counted among the blessed in the land—he does not give them over to the desire of their foes. The Lord sustains them on their sickbed and restores them from their bed of illness. Psalm 41:2-3*

My prayers, hopes, and dreams:

SPIRITUAL REVELATION

Let the following scripture speak to your heart as you meditate on it. Then, write down the things you hear God saying to you. God has a prophetic message for you. Hear it now!

In the same way, the Spirit helps us in our weakness. We do not know what we ought to pray for, but the Spirit himself intercedes for us through wordless groans. Romans 8:26

My spiritual insights and revelations:

Prayer No. 5

PROPHETIC PRAYER

*H*eavenly Father, I thank you for life itself and for the opportunity to know you as Lord. I thank you for letting me petition you for grace and mercy. Give me the mind to pray more often throughout my day. This is my heart's prayer.

Devote yourselves to prayer, being watchful and thankful. Colossians 4:2

My prayer for today:

PERSONAL REFLECTIONS

Look to God when your heart is broken. He will secure you. He will take the pain and turn it into joy! Only God can do that.

He heals the brokenhearted and binds up their wounds.
Psalm 147:3

My prayers, hopes, and dreams:

Spiritual Revelation

Let the following scripture speak to your heart as you meditate on it. Then, write down the things you hear God saying to you. God has a prophetic message for you. Hear it now!

I keep asking that the God of our Lord Jesus Christ, the glorious Father, may give you the Spirit of wisdom and revelation, so that you may know him better. Ephesians 1:17

My spiritual insights and revelations:

Prayer No. 6

PROPHETIC PRAYER

Dear God, I am tempted by the situations of life. They challenge my faith. But you, Lord, are bigger than them all. So be my strength when I am weak. Be my guide when I am lost. Be my joy when I am sad.

Watch and pray so that you will not fall into temptation. The spirit is willing, but the flesh is weak. Matthew 26:41

My prayer for today:

Personal Reflections

True rest can only come from a close relationship and fellowship with God. God is inviting you, now, to come to him for rest.

"Come to me, all you who are weary and burdened, and I will give you rest. Matthew 11:28

My prayers, hopes, and dreams:

SPIRITUAL REVELATION

Let the following scripture speak to your heart as you meditate on it. Then, write down the things you hear God saying to you. God has a prophetic message for you. Hear it now!

So he said to me, "This is the word of the Lord to Zerubbabel: 'Not by might nor by power, but by my Spirit,' says the Lord Almighty." Zechariah 4:6

My spiritual insights and revelations:

Prayer No. 7

PROPHETIC PRAYER

*M*ost high God, I come before you
with praise, honor, and a humble
heart. Hear me now as I enter into your
presence. I release my anger and frustration
so you can have your way in me.

---

*Therefore I want the men everywhere to
pray, lifting up holy hands without anger
or disputing. Timothy 2:8*

My prayer for today:

PERSONAL REFLECTIONS

Fear is normal, but it does not have to be defeating. Knowing that God is bigger than fear helps. God will keep you in times of trouble.

So do not fear, for I am with you; do not be dismayed, for I am your God. I will strengthen you and help you; I will uphold you with my righteous right hand.
Isaiah 41:10

My prayers, hopes, and dreams:

SPIRITUAL REVELATION

Let the following scripture speak to your heart as you meditate on it. Then, write down the things you hear God saying to you. God has a prophetic message for you. Hear it now!

For those who are led by the Spirit of God are the children of God. Romans 8:14

My spiritual insights and revelations:

Prayer No. 8

PROPHETIC PRAYER

*L*ord, I thank you for letting me seek you in prayer. Help me to pray without form or fashion, but plainly with purpose. Accept the words of my mouth and meditation of my heart. You know what I need. So meet it now.

And when you pray, do not keep on babbling like pagans, for they think they will be heard because of their many words. Do not be like them, for your Father knows what you need before you ask him. Matthew 6:7-8

My prayer for today:

PERSONAL REFLECTIONS

Prayer is not just a ritual; it is a route to God's power over circumstances. Prayer works! Expect it to work in your life.

Is anyone among you sick? Let them call the elders of the church to pray over them and anoint them with oil in the name of the Lord. James 5:14

My prayers, hopes, and dreams:

SPIRITUAL REVELATION

Let the following scripture speak to your heart as you meditate on it. Then, write down the things you hear God saying to you. God has a prophetic message for you. Hear it now!

And we all, who with unveiled faces contemplate the Lord's glory, are being transformed into his image with ever-increasing glory, which comes from the Lord, who is the Spirit.
2 Corinthians 3:18

My spiritual insights and revelations:

Prayer No. 9

PROPHETIC PRAYER

*G*od, I thank you for delivering me from sin and its constraints. You have redeemed me and given me an eternal home in heaven. My life has changed because of you. I am healed and whole.

Praise the Lord, my soul, and forget not all his benefits—who forgives all your sins and heals all your diseases, who redeems your life from the pit and crowns you with love and compassion. Psalm 103:2-4

My prayer for today:

Personal Reflections

It is important that you find the place and time to pray. Make if sooner than later. Be committed to a consistent prayer life.

Very early in the morning, while it was still dark, Jesus got up, left the house and went off to a solitary place, where he prayed.
Mark 1:35

My prayers, hopes, and dreams:

SPIRITUAL REVELATION

Let the following scripture speak to your heart as you meditate on it. Then, write down the things you hear God saying to you. God has a prophetic message for you. Hear it now!

If you then, though you are evil, know how to give good gifts to your children, how much more will your Father in heaven give the Holy Spirit to those who ask him! Luke 11:13

My spiritual insights and revelations:

Prayer No. 10

PROPHETIC PRAYER

*L*ord, when I find myself in need, no matter what it is, give me the strength to lean on you. Remind me that you are there with me and for me. I cannot make it without you. So meet my needs. Establish your presence in me.

And my God will meet all your needs according to the riches of his glory in Christ Jesus. Philippians 4:19

My prayer for today:

PERSONAL REFLECTIONS

The will of God is not always easy to complete. Prayer is important to preparation. With prayer, you will find the strength.

> *Going a little farther, he fell to the ground and prayed that if possible the hour might pass from him. "Abba, Father," he said, "everything is possible for you. Take this cup from me. Yet not what I will, but what you will."*
> Mark 14:35-36

My prayers, hopes, and dreams:

Spiritual Revelation

Let the following scripture speak to your heart as you meditate on it. Then, write down the things you hear God saying to you. God has a prophetic message for you. Hear it now!

They saw what seemed to be tongues of fire that separated and came to rest on each of them. All of them were filled with the Holy Spirit and began to speak in other tongues as the Spirit enabled them. Acts 2:3-4

My spiritual insights and revelations:

Prayer No. 11

PROPHETIC PRAYER

*L*ord, when I come to you, let me spend time with you. Let me sit in your presence until you answer my call. Whether it is a short day or a long night, I will remain faithful in my prayers.

One of those days Jesus went out to a mountainside to pray, and spent the night praying to God. Luke 6:12

My prayer for today:

Personal Reflections

Healing is the divine plan of God for your life. One route to healing is through forgiveness of sin. Don't let your current situation keep you from your best life before God. Ask him to heal you.

Praise the Lord, my soul, and forget not all his benefits—who forgives all your sins and heals all your diseases. Psalm 103:2-3

My prayers, hopes, and dreams:

SPIRITUAL REVELATION

Let the following scripture speak to your heart as you meditate on it. Then, write down the things you hear God saying to you. God has a prophetic message for you. Hear it now!

The Spirit himself testifies with our spirit that we are God's children.
Romans 8:16

My spiritual insights and revelations:

Prayer No. 12

PROPHETIC PRAYER

Lord, help me to forgive those that have wronged me. And not only that Lord, help those that I have wronged to forgive me. Lord, I need your forgiveness. And I thank you for hearing my plea today.

And when you stand praying, if you hold anything against anyone, forgive them, so that your Father in heaven may forgive you your sins. Mark 11:25

My prayer for today:

PERSONAL REFLECTIONS

It doesn't matter how long you have been in your condition. Neither does it matter what the condition is, God can heal you. Faith makes it possible for you to be healed. Activate your faith and experience the miracle. Hallelujah!

And a woman was there who had been subject to bleeding for twelve years, but no one could heal her. She came up behind him and touched the edge of his cloak, and immediately her bleeding stopped. Luke 8:43-44

Then he said to her, "Daughter, your faith has healed you. Go in peace." Luke 8:48

My prayers, hopes, and dreams:

SPIRITUAL REVELATION

Let the following scripture speak to your heart as you meditate on it. Then, write down the things you hear God saying to you. God has a prophetic message for you. Hear it now!

For the flesh desires what is contrary to the Spirit, and the Spirit what is contrary to the flesh. They are in conflict with each other, so that you are not to do whatever you want.
Galatians 5:17

My spiritual insights and revelations:

Prayer No. 13

PROPHETIC PRAYER

Father God, give me the courage to stand in agreement for emotional healing with those around me. And Lord, bless me with friendships that will help keep me in favor with you.

Therefore confess your sins to each other and pray for each other so that you may be healed. The prayer of a righteous person is powerful and effective. James 5:16

My prayer for today:

Personal Reflections

God will protect you from the conditions around you. Whether the conditions are natural or man-made, God has a protection plan. All he asks is that you obey his commands.

> *He said, "If you listen carefully to the Lord your God and do what is right in his eyes, if you pay attention to his commands and keep all his decrees, I will not bring on you any of the diseases I brought on the Egyptians, for I am the Lord, who heals you."*
> *Exodus 15:26*

My prayers, hopes, and dreams:

SPIRITUAL REVELATION

Let the following scripture speak to your heart as you meditate on it. Then, write down the things you hear God saying to you. God has a prophetic message for you. Hear it now!

Make every effort to keep the unity of the Spirit through the bond of peace. Ephesians 4:3

My spiritual insights and revelations:

Prayer No. 14

PROPHETIC PRAYER

Lord, you are the Sovereign God. You are the one and only creator of all. You are the one that I acknowledge when I pray and worship. You are the great King who orchestrates it all, on earth and in heaven. And for that I praise you. Help me to continue to praise you daily!

On their release, Peter and John went back to their own people and reported all that the chief priests and the elders had said to them. When they heard this, they raised their voices together in prayer to God. "Sovereign Lord," they said, "you made the heavens and the earth and the sea, and everything in them. Acts 4:23-24

My prayer for today:

PERSONAL REFLECTIONS

You may have issues and problems from your past. But that past is no match for the power of God. God is a deliverer. He is a way maker. Trust him to keep you from life's harms.

> *The Lord will keep you free from every disease. He will not inflict on you the horrible diseases you knew in Egypt, but he will inflict them on all who hate you.*
> *Deuteronomy 7:15*

My prayers, hopes, and dreams:

Spiritual Revelation

Let the following scripture speak to your heart as you meditate on it. Then, write down the things you hear God saying to you. God has a prophetic message for you. Hear it now!

In the beginning God created the heavens and the earth. Now the earth was formless and empty, darkness was over the surface of the deep, and the Spirit of God was hovering over the waters. Genesis 1:1-2

My spiritual insights and revelations:

Prayer No. 15

PROPHETIC PRAYER

*D*ear Lord, as I call out to you, I know you hear the hopelessness in every breath. I also know that you will not leave me in my current state. So I thank you in advance for my deliverance. Thank you for not being deaf to my concerns.

"Hear my prayer, Lord, listen to my cry for help; do not be deaf to my weeping. I dwell with you as a foreigner, a stranger, as all my ancestors were. Psalm 39:12

My prayer for today:

Personal Reflections

When problems arise, call on the Lord to bring you out of them. He is standing by right now to do whatever you ask. He loves you and wants the best for you. He will rescue you.

Then they cried to the Lord in their trouble, he saved them from their distress. He sent out his word and healed them; rescued them from the grave. Let them give thanks to the Lord for his unfailing love and his wonderful deeds for mankind.
Psalm 107:19-21

My prayers, hopes, and dreams:

SPIRITUAL REVELATION

Let the following scripture speak to your heart as you meditate on it. Then, write down the things you hear God saying to you. God has a prophetic message for you. Hear it now!

For I know that through your prayers and God's provision of the Spirit of Jesus Christ what has happened to me will turn out for my deliverance. Philippians 1:19

My spiritual insights and revelations:

Prayer No. 16

PROPHETIC PRAYER

*L*ord, I come near to you with childlike confidence to pray on behalf of those with whom I have contact. I pray that they might not be troubled within. I pray there be no disturbance in their spirit. Grant them favor and create godliness within them.

I urge, then, first of all, that petitions, prayers, intercession and thanksgiving be made for all people—for kings and all those in authority, that we may live peaceful and quiet lives in all godliness and holiness. 1 Timothy 2:1-2

My prayer for today:

Personal Reflections

It is wonderful to ask God for something and see it happen. No matter how often you need him, God will answer you. Ask him now to heal your body and mind, and restore your joy.

Lord my God, I called to you for help, and you healed me. Psalm 30:2

My prayers, hopes, and dreams:

SPIRITUAL REVELATION

Let the following scripture speak to your heart as you meditate on it. Then, write down the things you hear God saying to you. God has a prophetic message for you. Hear it now!

Do you not know that your bodies are temples of the Holy Spirit, who is in you, whom you have received from God? You are not your own; you were bought at a price. Therefore honor God with your bodies. 1 Corinthians 6:19-20

My spiritual insights and revelations:

Prayer No. 17

PROPHETIC PRAYER

*D*ear Lord, you have brought your peace to my family. It has blessed us to have a safe place. Thank you. Your peace continues to bless me. I love you because of what you do for me and who you are in my life.

Pray for the peace of Jerusalem! May they be secure who love you! Psalm 122:6

My prayer for today:

PERSONAL REFLECTIONS

God has his eye on you. He sees the distress you are in. He will deliver you from it. When he does, those around you will see how powerful his hand is upon your life. God will elevate you.

You have delivered me from the attacks of the people; you have made me the head of nations. People I did not know now serve me. Psalm 18:43

My prayers, hopes, and dreams:

SPIRITUAL REVELATION

Let the following scripture speak to your heart as you meditate on it. Then, write down the things you hear God saying to you. God has a prophetic message for you. Hear it now!

> *Peter replied, "Repent and be baptized, every one of you, in the name of Jesus Christ for the forgiveness of your sins. And you will receive the gift of the Holy Spirit." Acts 2:38*

My spiritual insights and revelations:

Prayer No. 18

PROPHETIC PRAYER

*L*ord, you are so gracious and kind to hear my prayer and respond to my need. Give me wisdom and strength as I keep moving towards you. I believe I am more than a conqueror. I am a winner! Save me in my time of need.

Save us, we pray, O Lord! O Lord, we pray, give us success! Psalm 118:25

My prayer for today:

Personal Reflections

What God does for you will be complete. You will see and experience the effect of his healing. He sees you offering praise up to him. He takes delight in it and will reward you.

> *Heal me, Lord, and I will be healed; save me and I will be saved, for you are the one I praise. Jeremiah 17:14*

My prayers, hopes, and dreams:

SPIRITUAL REVELATION

Let the following scripture speak to your heart as you meditate on it. Then, write down the things you hear God saying to you. God has a prophetic message for you. Hear it now!

When he and his servant arrived at Gibeah, a procession of prophets met him; the Spirit of God came powerfully upon him, and he joined in their prophesying. 1 Samuel 10:10

My spiritual insights and revelations:

Prayer No. 19

PROPHETIC PRAYER

*L*ord, what a great display of your grace to allow me to seek you. You invite me to come to you in prayer, to seek your will and your promises. So Lord, help me to persevere as I ask in prayer for your will for my life. I knock expecting the door to be opened.

Ask, and it will be given to you seek, and you will find; knock, and it will be opened to you. Matthew 7:7

My prayer for today:

PERSONAL REFLECTIONS

God has promised to answer you when you call on him. Whether you call in peace or in trouble, the same God will answer. God wants to show himself to be true to his word. Let him!

He will call on me, and I will answer him; I will be with him in trouble, I will deliver him and honor him. With long life I will satisfy him and show him my salvation." Psalm 91:15-16

My prayers, hopes, and dreams:

SPIRITUAL REVELATION

Let the following scripture speak to your heart as you meditate on it. Then, write down the things you hear God saying to you. God has a prophetic message for you. Hear it now!

The Spirit of God has made me; the breath of the Almighty gives me life. Job 33:4

My spiritual insights and revelations:

Prayer No. 20

PROPHETIC PRAYER

*L*ord, I am thankful for faith in you and the works of your hand. I am thankful for the right to come to you to fulfill my needs. As I do so, I am blessed by you. My needs are met in you. Thank you.

And whatever you ask in prayer, you will receive, if you have faith." Matthew 21:22

My prayer for today:

PERSONAL REFLECTIONS

Jesus Christ is the agent of your complete healing. Jesus is the one who took on the pains of healing so that you would not have to. Confessing Jesus brings about healing. Confess Jesus now and receive the blessing!

Surely he took up our pain and bore our suffering, yet we considered him punished by God, stricken by him, and afflicted. But he was pierced for our transgressions, he was crushed for our iniquities; the punishment that brought us peace was on him, and by his wounds we are healed. Isaiah 53:4-5

My prayers, hopes, and dreams:

SPIRITUAL REVELATION

Let the following scripture speak to your heart as you meditate on it. Then, write down the things you hear God saying to you. God has a prophetic message for you. Hear it now!

> *Create in me a pure heart, O God, and renew a steadfast spirit within me. Do not cast me from your presence or take your Holy Spirit from me. Restore to me the joy of your salvation and grant me a willing spirit, to sustain me. Psalm 51:10-12*

My spiritual insights and revelations:

Prayer No. 21

PROPHETIC PRAYER

*I*ndescribable and incomparable God, thank you for permitting me to petition you for help. In knowing who you are, I receive an abundant overflow of blessings each time that I ask. I am now asking you to meet me in this time of need.

Therefore I tell you, whatever you ask in prayer, believe that you have received it, and it will be yours. Mark 11:24

My prayer for today:

PERSONAL REFLECTIONS

Jesus is the healer of mankind. He is also a great teacher. With healing and teaching comes the freedom to live a life of physical comfort and emotional peace. Receive Jesus.

Jesus went through all the towns and villages, teaching in their synagogues, proclaiming the good news of the kingdom and healing every disease and sickness. Matthew 9:35

My prayers, hopes, and dreams:

SPIRITUAL REVELATION

Let the following scripture speak to your heart as you meditate on it. Then, write down the things you hear God saying to you. God has a prophetic message for you. Hear it now!

When you send your Spirit, they are created, and you renew the face of the ground. Psalm 104:30

My spiritual insights and revelations:

Prayer No. 22

PROPHETIC PRAYER

*L*ord Jesus, you are truly a marvelous caretaker and a wonderful giver of hope. You have made yourself available to me. Your name shows greatness and honor. Thank you for permission to seek God's favor in your name.

Whatever you ask in my name, this I will do, that the Father may be glorified in the Son. If you ask me anything in my name, I will do it. John 14:13-14

My prayer for today:

PERSONAL REFLECTIONS

Sin will keep you from a relationship with God, including eternity in heaven. But when you acknowledge God, he erases the consequences of sin. He treats you as though the sin never occurred.

"I, even I, am he who blots out your transgressions, for my own sake, and remembers your sins no more. Isaiah 43:25

My prayers, hopes, and dreams:

SPIRITUAL REVELATION

Let the following scripture speak to your heart as you meditate on it. Then, write down the things you hear God saying to you. God has a prophetic message for you. Hear it now!

Teach me to do your will, for you are my God; may your good Spirit lead me on level ground.
Psalm 143:10

My spiritual insights and revelations:

Prayer No. 23

PROPHETIC PRAYER

*L*ord, you are so loving and caring that you have given us elders to intercede on our behalf. Let your will be done through them as they invite your anointed power into the lives of those in need. Help me also to become an intercessor on behalf of others.

Is anyone among you sick? Let him call for the elders of the church, and let them pray over him, anointing him with oil in the name of the Lord. And the prayer of faith will save the one who is sick, and the Lord will raise him up. And if he has committed sins, he will be forgiven. James 5:14-15

My prayer for today:

PERSONAL REFLECTIONS

Faith is a powerful weapon against the circumstances of life that are controlling you. By faith, God will grant healing. With healing comes peace because you are freed from the physical, emotional or spiritual constraints.

He said to her, "Daughter, your faith has healed you. Go in peace and be freed from your suffering." Mark 5:34

My prayers, hopes, and dreams:

SPIRITUAL REVELATION

Let the following scripture speak to your heart as you meditate on it. Then, write down the things you hear God saying to you. God has a prophetic message for you. Hear it now!

He will be a spirit of justice to the one who sits in judgment, a source of strength to those who turn back the battle at the gate. Isaiah 28:6

My spiritual insights and revelations:

Prayer No. 24

PROPHETIC PRAYER

*D*ear Lord, teach me not to be anxious about life's situations or be troubled by circumstances that come upon me. Instead, let me continue in earnest prayer with a peaceful and thankful heart to believe the promises given through Christ Jesus.

Do not be anxious about anything, but in everything by prayer and supplication with thanksgiving let your requests be made known to God. And the peace of God, which surpasses all understanding, will guard your hearts and your minds in Christ Jesus. Philippians 4:6-7

My prayer for today:

PERSONAL REFLECTIONS

God's plan is for you to lead the world, not follow the "worldly" ways. Obeying God makes it possible for you to take your rightful position as the head. He will bless whatever you do.

> *If you fully obey the Lord your God and carefully follow all his commands I give you today, the Lord your God will set you high above all the nations on earth. All these blessings will come on you and accompany you if you obey the Lord your God.*
> *Deuteronomy 28:1-2*

My prayers, hopes, and dreams:

SPIRITUAL REVELATION

Let the following scripture speak to your heart as you meditate on it. Then, write down the things you hear God saying to you. God has a prophetic message for you. Hear it now!

> *"As for me, this is my covenant with them," says the Lord. "My Spirit, who is on you, will not depart from you, and my words that I have put in your mouth will always be on your lips, on the lips of your children and on the lips of their descendants—from this time on and forever," says the Lord. Isaiah 59:21*

My spiritual insights and revelations:

Prayer No. 25

PROPHETIC PRAYER

*A*lmighty and Holy God, help me not to ramble when I seek you, but to be simple and direct with my plead. Let me know that when I ask in prayer and believe by faith that the answer is already given.

Therefore I tell you, whatever you ask in prayer, believe that you have received it, and it will be yours. Mark 11:24

My prayer for today:

PERSONAL REFLECTIONS

What is impossible for you, is possible for God. His son, Jesus, is the agent through whom you can experience your miracle. Don't be distracted by the unbelief of others. Believe and you will receive. God's blessings are waiting.

> *Meanwhile, all the people were wailing and mourning for her. "Stop wailing," Jesus said. "She is not dead but asleep." They laughed at him, knowing that she was dead. But he took her by the hand and said, "My child, get up!" Her spirit returned, and at once she stood up. Then Jesus told them to give her something to eat. Luke 8:52-55*

My prayers, hopes, and dreams:

SPIRITUAL REVELATION

Let the following scripture speak to your heart as you meditate on it. Then, write down the things you hear God saying to you. God has a prophetic message for you. Hear it now!

> "I baptize you with water for repentance. But after me comes one who is more powerful than I, whose sandals I am not worthy to carry. He will baptize you with the Holy Spirit and fire. Matthew 3:11

My spiritual insights and revelations:

Prayer No. 26

PROPHETIC PRAYER

*L*ord God, I expressed my thoughts to you as I go throughout the day. Often, it's with words of sorrow and groans from my soul. Thank you for acknowledging the sound of my cry. I need you each hour of the day. Please hear me now.

Evening and morning and at noon I utter my complaint and moan, and he hears my voice. Psalm 55:17

My prayer for today:

PERSONAL REFLECTIONS

Sometimes the many circumstances of life will cause you to become anxious about the outcomes. But there is peace that comes with knowing Jesus. Your emotions are more stable with Jesus in your life. Pray about it to him today.

Do not be anxious about anything, but in every situation, by prayer and petition, with thanksgiving, present your requests to God. And the peace of God, which transcends all understanding, will guard your hearts and your minds in Christ Jesus. Philippians 4:6-7

My prayers, hopes, and dreams:

SPIRITUAL REVELATION

Let the following scripture speak to your heart as you meditate on it. Then, write down the things you hear God saying to you. God has a prophetic message for you. Hear it now!

Jesus answered, "Very truly I tell you, no one can enter the kingdom of God unless they are born of water and the Spirit. Flesh gives birth to flesh, but the Spirit gives birth to spirit. John 3:5-6

My spiritual insights and revelations:

Prayer No. 27

PROPHETIC PRAYER

*F*ather, I greet you with anticipation of my time with you. As I seek you with my morning sacrifices, let your presence spring forth and refresh my soul.

But I, O Lord, cry to you; in the morning my prayer comes before you.
Psalm 88:13

My prayer for today:

PERSONAL REFLECTIONS

God is a comforter to all who seek him. He sees your sorrow and he knows your pain. He will not let you continue to feel down about life. And, in the end, he will grant you eternal life.

'He will wipe every tear from their eyes. There will be no more death' or mourning or crying or pain, for the old order of things has passed away." Revelation 21:4

My prayers, hopes, and dreams:

SPIRITUAL REVELATION

Let the following scripture speak to your heart as you meditate on it. Then, write down the things you hear God saying to you. God has a prophetic message for you. Hear it now!

The Spirit gives life; the flesh counts for nothing. The words I have spoken to you—they are full of the Spirit and life. John 6:63

My spiritual insights and revelations:

Prayer No. 28

PROPHETIC PRAYER

Father, as I sit in my private place where no ear can hear me but yours, and no eyes can see me but yours, I shall not be moved. I anticipate your presence and the promise of my reward from you.

But when you pray, go into your room and shut the door and pray to your Father who is in secret. And your Father who sees in secret will reward you."
Matthew 6:6

My prayer for today:

PERSONAL REFLECTIONS

Not only do you need healing, so do those around you. Help them by introducing them to Jesus. He wants to heal them too, no matter their circumstance. God cares for all. Bring them to Jesus and see the difference it makes.

Crowds gathered also from the towns around Jerusalem, bringing their sick and those tormented by impure spirits, and all of them were healed.
Acts 5:16

My prayers, hopes, and dreams:

SPIRITUAL REVELATION

Let the following scripture speak to your heart as you meditate on it. Then, write down the things you hear God saying to you. God has a prophetic message for you. Hear it now!

But you will receive power when the Holy Spirit comes on you; and you will be my witnesses in Jerusalem, and in all Judea and Samaria, and to the ends of the earth." Acts 1:8

My spiritual insights and revelations:

Prayer No. 29

PROPHETIC PRAYER

*L*ord, thank you for the Holy Spirit who holds me up when I have no strength to properly petition you. I know the Holy Spirit has the power to speak for me when my language falls short. Thank you for hearing my plea even when I can't express myself.

Likewise the Spirit helps us in our weakness. For we do not know what to pray for as we ought, but the Spirit himself intercedes for us with groanings too deep for words." Romans 8:26

My prayer for today:

PERSONAL REFLECTIONS

When you accept God into your life, through Jesus, you gain access to the power of God. Therefore, you can petition God for miraculous changes around you. Ask him now. There is power in the name of Jesus!

And these signs will accompany those who believe: In my name they will drive out demons; they will speak in new tongues; they will pick up snakes with their hands; and when they drink deadly poison, it will not hurt them at all; they will place their hands on sick people, and they will get well." Mark 16:17-18

My prayers, hopes, and dreams:

SPIRITUAL REVELATION

Let the following scripture speak to your heart as you meditate on it. Then, write down the things you hear God saying to you. God has a prophetic message for you. Hear it now!

But the Advocate, the Holy Spirit, whom the Father will send in my name, will teach you all things and will remind you of everything I have said to you.
John 14:26

My spiritual insights and revelations:

Prayer No. 30

PROPHETIC PRAYER

*P*recious Lord, I have called upon you and you have heard me. You have given me relief from my pain. You have quieted my soul. I am so grateful that you heard my prayer and encouraged me with your divine goodness.

Answer me when I call, O God of my righteousness! You have given me relief when I was in distress. Be gracious to me and hear my prayer! Psalm 4:1

My prayer for today:

PERSONAL REFLECTIONS

In the world, there will always be the possibility of victory or defeat, life or death. God grants you the mind to believe and receive the best. That means life. So live it!

> *This day I call the heavens and the earth as witnesses against you that I have set before you life and death, blessings and curses. Now choose life, so that you and your children may live and that you may love the Lord your God, listen to his voice, and hold fast to him. For the Lord is your life, and he will give you many years in the land he swore to give to your fathers, Abraham, Isaac and Jacob.*
> *Deuteronomy 30:19-20*

My prayers, hopes, and dreams:

SPIRITUAL REVELATION

Let the following scripture speak to your heart as you meditate on it. Then, write down the things you hear God saying to you. God has a prophetic message for you. Hear it now!

And I myself did not know him, but the one who sent me to baptize with water told me, 'The man on whom you see the Spirit come down and remain is the one who will baptize with the Holy Spirit.' John 1:33

My spiritual insights and revelations:

Prayer No. 31

PROPHETIC PRAYER

*S*overeign Lord, I come to your altar to pray. I exalt your name above every name. Help me continue to show love, joy and peace in the midst of confusion. Be my strength.

"I desire then that in every place the men should pray, lifting holy hands without anger or quarreling;" 1 Timothy 2:8

My prayer for today:

PERSONAL REFLECTIONS

There may be times when all seems lost. But all is not lost when you have God in your life. No matter what you lost, God can restore it. It doesn't matter what others think of you. God intends to bless you. You will recover.

But I will restore you to health and heal your wounds,' declares the Lord, 'because you are called an outcast, Zion for whom no one cares. Jeremiah 30:17

My prayers, hopes, and dreams:

SPIRITUAL REVELATION

Let the following scripture speak to your heart as you meditate on it. Then, write down the things you hear God saying to you. God has a prophetic message for you. Hear it now!

> *Whenever you are arrested and brought to trial, do not worry beforehand about what to say. Just say whatever is given you at the time, for it is not you speaking, but the Holy Spirit*
> *Mark 13:11*

My spiritual insights and revelations:

Prayer No. 32

PROPHETIC PRAYER

Almighty and eternal God, I come to you with boldness and no hesitation, no restraints, or negativity. I come with a positive mindset knowing that you will grant my request according to your magnificent will.

"And this is the confidence that we have toward him, that if we ask anything according to his will he hears us. And if we know that he hears us in whatever we ask, we know that we have the requests that we have asked of him." 1 John 5:14-15

My prayer for today:

PERSONAL REFLECTIONS

Sickness and poor health, aches and pains will happen. But Jesus is willing to heal you from them all. Don't let depression, sadness or apathy keep you from being healed. Ask Jesus. He is the difference maker for healing!

> *A man with leprosy came and knelt before him and said, "Lord, if you are willing, you can make me clean." Jesus reached out his hand and touched the man. "I am willing," he said. "Be clean!" Immediately he was cleansed of his leprosy. Matthew 8:2-3*

My prayers, hopes, and dreams:

SPIRITUAL REVELATION

Let the following scripture speak to your heart as you meditate on it. Then, write down the things you hear God saying to you. God has a prophetic message for you. Hear it now!

We are witnesses of these things, and so is the Holy Spirit, whom God has given to those who obey him. Acts 5:32

My spiritual insights and revelations:

Prayer No. 33

PROPHETIC PRAYER

*L*ord, what great comfort it is to know that you hear my petition. You not only hear the petition of my heart, but you listen to the words from my mouth. I utter words with great anticipation of your reward.

Hear my prayer, O God; listen to the words of my mouth. Psalm 54:2

My prayer for today:

PERSONAL REFLECTIONS

Doubt will rob you of your healing. It will confine you to a poor state. But it is time for you to believe that you can speak to your circumstance and it will change. Speak to it now!

Jesus replied, "Truly I tell you, if you have faith and do not doubt, not only can you do what was done to the fig tree, but also you can say to this mountain, 'Go, throw yourself into the sea,' and it will be done. Matthew 21:21

My prayers, hopes, and dreams:

Spiritual Revelation

Let the following scripture speak to your heart as you meditate on it. Then, write down the things you hear God saying to you. God has a prophetic message for you. Hear it now!

So again I ask, does God give you his Spirit and work miracles among you by the works of the law, or by your believing what you heard? Galatians 3:5

My spiritual insights and revelations:

Prayer No. 34

PROPHETIC PRAYER

Gracious and generous God, you are the giver of all good gifts. You know my needs before I bring them to you. And you have faithfully carried me from the womb and have promised to carry me through any problems I may encounter. I ask for your wisdom and deliverance so I can faithfully serve you in all things.

"Listen to me, you descendants of Jacob, all the remnant of the people of Israel, you whom I have upheld since your birth, and have carried since you were born. Even to your old age and gray hairs I am he, I am he who will sustain you. I have made you and I will carry you; I will sustain you and I will rescue you. Isaiah 46:3-4

My prayer for today:

PERSONAL REFLECTIONS

God truly is the same yesterday, today, and forever. He will deliver on whatever he promises. What you've seen him do for others, he is ready to do for you. Just follow his word!

> *"Praise be to the Lord, who has given rest to his people Israel just as he promised. Not one word has failed of all the good promises he gave through his servant Moses. May the Lord our God be with us as he was with our ancestors; may he never leave us nor forsake us. May he turn our hearts to him, to walk in obedience to him and keep the commands, decrees and laws he gave our ancestors. 1 Kings 8:56-58*

My prayers, hopes, and dreams:

Spiritual Revelation

Let the following scripture speak to your heart as you meditate on it. Then, write down the things you hear God saying to you. God has a prophetic message for you. Hear it now!

Therefore, with minds that are alert and fully sober, set your hope on the grace to be brought to you when Jesus Christ is revealed at his coming. 1 Peter 1:13

My spiritual insights and revelations:

Prayer No. 35

PROPHETIC PRAYER

Father of all nations, I will always let my prayers be made unto you. Let me be driven to approach you with my love so that you will be guided toward me with a helping hand when you hear my heart's prayer.

But I pray to you, Lord, in the time of your favor; in your great love, O God, answer me with your sure salvation.
Psalm 69:13

My prayer for today:

Personal Reflections

God keeps his word. No matter what he says, it is true. Therefore, you can be assured that the things he has said in your favor will happen. You can trust God. His word is faithful.

I will not violate my covenant or alter what my lips have uttered.
Psalm 89:34

My prayers, hopes, and dreams:

SPIRITUAL REVELATION

Let the following scripture speak to your heart as you meditate on it. Then, write down the things you hear God saying to you. God has a prophetic message for you. Hear it now!

The one who keeps God's commands lives in him, and he in them. And this is how we know that he lives in us: We know it by the Spirit he gave us. 1 John 3:24

My spiritual insights and revelations:

Prayer No. 36

PROPHETIC PRAYER

Heavenly father, I cry out to you. I seek compassion and forgiveness in my time of need.

Hear my prayer, Lord; listen to my cry for mercy. Psalm 86:6

My prayer for today:

PERSONAL REFLECTIONS

Miracles are under the authority of Jesus. And when you are under Jesus, miracles are at your disposal. You can then command problems and issues to be removed from you. Your prayer life will become your miraculous life.

> *"Truly I tell you, if anyone says to this mountain, 'Go, throw yourself into the sea,' and does not doubt in their heart but believes that what they say will happen, it will be done for them. Therefore I tell you, whatever you ask for in prayer, believe that you have received it, and it will be yours. Mark 11:23-24*

My prayers, hopes, and dreams:

SPIRITUAL REVELATION

Let the following scripture speak to your heart as you meditate on it. Then, write down the things you hear God saying to you. God has a prophetic message for you. Hear it now!

Whoever sows to please their flesh, from the flesh will reap destruction; whoever sows to please the Spirit, from the Spirit will reap eternal life.
Galatians 6:8

My spiritual insights and revelations:

Prayer No. 37

PROPHETIC PRAYER

*J*ehovah God, I thank you for not passing me over while I was in a place of poverty. You did not turn from me, but instead, you turned toward me when you heard my plea. For that, I am grateful.

He will respond to the prayer of the destitute; he will not despise their plea.
Psalm 102:17

My prayer for today:

PERSONAL REFLECTIONS

At some point in life, you will find yourself
under distress. You might be there right now.
When it happens, remember to call on God.
He is standing by waiting to deliver you. You
don't have to stay down. God will lift you up
to a better state!

*Then they cried to the Lord in
their trouble, and he saved them
from their distress. He sent out
his word and healed them; he
rescued them from the grave.
Psalm 107:19-20*

My prayers, hopes, and dreams:

SPIRITUAL REVELATION

Let the following scripture speak to your heart as you meditate on it. Then, write down the things you hear God saying to you. God has a prophetic message for you. Hear it now!

> *When the day of Pentecost came, they were all together in one place. Suddenly a sound like the blowing of a violent wind came from heaven and filled the whole house where they were sitting. Acts 2:1-2*

My spiritual insights and revelations:

Prayer No. 38

PROPHETIC PRAYER

To the all-knowing and compassionate God, you always recognize my cry without me uttering a word. Uphold me with your righteousness so that I am released from the torment and pain in my body and from the pursuit of my enemies.

Lord, hear my prayer, listen to my cry for mercy; in your faithfulness and righteousness come to my relief. Psalm 143:1

My prayer for today:

Personal Reflections

God has power and God has authority. And because of his love for you, he allows you to use it against your problems. So when you are under attack, you must activate your right to the power of God to defeat your enemies.

> *I have given you authority to trample on snakes and scorpions and to overcome all the power of the enemy; nothing will harm you. Luke 10:19*

My prayers, hopes, and dreams:

Spiritual Revelation

Let the following scripture speak to your heart as you meditate on it. Then, write down the things you hear God saying to you. God has a prophetic message for you. Hear it now!

There is one body and one Spirit, just as you were called to one hope when you were called.
Ephesians 4:4

My spiritual insights and revelations:

Prayer No. 39

PROPHETIC PRAYER

*H*eavenly Father, I appeal to you for directions and clarity that your right hand will appoint me to the place I must go. Thank you for granting me the understanding of how to work out things by your guidance. I am blessed by you.

Pray that the Lord your God will tell us where we should go and what we should do." Jeremiah 42:3

My prayer for today:

PERSONAL REFLECTIONS

Facing physical illnesses and issues can leave you in despair. In those times, exercise your faith against the problem and see God move. Proclaim your victory, even when it seems a long way off.

> *The Lord's right hand is lifted high; the Lord's right hand has done mighty things!" I will not die but live, and will proclaim what the Lord has done. Psalm 118:16-17*

My prayers, hopes, and dreams:

SPIRITUAL REVELATION

Let the following scripture speak to your heart as you meditate on it. Then, write down the things you hear God saying to you. God has a prophetic message for you. Hear it now!

Create in me a pure heart, O God, and renew a steadfast spirit within me. Psalm 51:10

My spiritual insights and revelations:

Prayer No. 40

PROPHETIC PRAYER

*L*ord God, what a privilege it is to know that I can come to you just as I am, without false pretenses. When I am in your presence, see my true heart without ulterior motives. See me as sincere when I pray. Be the God of my life.

And when you pray, do not be like the hypocrites, for they love to pray standing in the synagogues and on the street corners to be seen by others. Truly I tell you, they have received their reward in full. Matthew 6:5

My prayer for today:

PERSONAL REFLECTIONS

The struggles of life are real. They can come at you and leave you feeling like a loser. But you are not a loser. Jesus has bigger and better plans for your life. Life is to be lived not feared.

The thief comes only to steal and kill and destroy; I have come that they may have life, and have it to the full. John 10:10

My prayers, hopes, and dreams:

SPIRITUAL REVELATION

Let the following scripture speak to your heart as you meditate on it. Then, write down the things you hear God saying to you. God has a prophetic message for you. Hear it now!

And if the Spirit of him who raised Jesus from the dead is living in you, he who raised Christ from the dead will also give life to your mortal bodies because of his Spirit who lives in you. Romans 8:11

My spiritual insights and revelations:

Prayer No. 41

PROPHETIC PRAYER

*F*ather, sometimes I am not able to lift my head in my season of distress, even though I respect you as Lord. So please hear my plea and keep me strong. Act according to your divine will and purpose for my life. I thank you in advance.

Going a little farther, he fell with his face to the ground and prayed, "My Father, if it is possible, may this cup be taken from me. Yet not as I will, but as you will."

Matthew 26:39

My prayer for today:

PERSONAL REFLECTIONS

As good as you are at figuring things out, there is still no match for the wisdom of God. Trust him to give you the answers you need to succeed. Move towards your destiny on his path. And remember to thank him as you go.

Trust in the Lord with all your heart and lean not on your own understanding; 6 in all your ways submit to him, and he will make your paths straight. Proverbs 3:5

My prayers, hopes, and dreams:

SPIRITUAL REVELATION

Let the following scripture speak to your heart as you meditate on it. Then, write down the things you hear God saying to you. God has a prophetic message for you. Hear it now!

But you will receive power when the Holy Spirit comes on you; and you will be my witnesses in Jerusalem, and in all Judea and Samaria, and to the ends of the earth. Acts 1:8

My spiritual insights and revelations:

Prayer No. 42

PROPHETIC PRAYER

*L*ord God, your word teaches that you are gracious, merciful, and just in sharing blessings. Your word also teaches that sometimes I have to wait for those blessings to come. As I wait, I submit fully to your lordship. Please sustain me as I strive to live each moment according to your divine purpose.

In the same way, the Spirit helps us in our weakness. We do not know what we ought to pray for, but the Spirit himself intercedes for us through wordless groans.
Romans 8:26

My prayer for today:

PERSONAL REFLECTIONS

The circumstances of life can drain you to the point that you lose motivation for life itself. That is why you need Jesus in your life. Jesus will infuse your life with his power. He will restore your spirit by his spirit.

And if the Spirit of him who raised Jesus from the dead is living in you, he who raised Christ from the dead will also give life to your mortal bodies because of his Spirit who lives in you.
Romans 8:11

My prayers, hopes, and dreams:

SPIRITUAL REVELATION

Let the following scripture speak to your heart as you meditate on it. Then, write down the things you hear God saying to you. God has a prophetic message for you. Hear it now!

The soothing tongue is a tree of life, but a perverse tongue crushes the spirit. Proverbs 15:4

My spiritual insights and revelations:

Prayer No. 43

PROPHETIC PRAYER

*L*ord, I am rejoicing in prayer as I am preserved through life's tribulations. Let me find the spirit of endurance so I may continue to exercise my faith.

Be joyful in hope, patient in affliction, faithful in prayer. Romans 12:12

My prayer for today:

PERSONAL REFLECTIONS

Your total well-being matters to God. God wants your spiritual, emotional, social, and even financial life to be a success. Let total healing become your goal. Ask God to grant it to you so you can enjoy your life. God will grant it.

Dear friend, I pray that you may enjoy good health and that all may go well with you, even as your soul is getting along well.
3 John 2

My prayers, hopes, and dreams:

Spiritual Revelation

Let the following scripture speak to your heart as you meditate on it. Then, write down the things you hear God saying to you. God has a prophetic message for you. Hear it now!

For our struggle is not against flesh and blood, but against the rulers, against the authorities, against the powers of this dark world and against the spiritual forces of evil in the heavenly realms. Ephesians 6:12

My spiritual insights and revelations:

Prayer No. 44

PROPHETIC PRAYER

*M*erciful Lord, your word declares that I should not do things only for myself, but for others as well. Don't let the enemy tempt me to forget about the needs of others as I take care of my own. Help me to be a blessing to others, as I am blessed by you.

Do nothing out of selfish ambition or vain conceit. Rather, in humility value others above yourselves, not looking to your own interests but each of you to the interests of the others. Philippians 2:3-4

My prayer for today:

PERSONAL REFLECTIONS

Situations and life itself can leave you feeling weak and disappointed. Then concerns can set in about the future. But God says that he is with you. He will lift you up and establish you.

So do not fear, for I am with you; do not be dismayed, for I am your God. I will strengthen you and help you; I will uphold you with my righteous right hand.
Isaiah 41:10

My prayers, hopes, and dreams:

Spiritual Revelation

Let the following scripture speak to your heart as you meditate on it. Then, write down the things you hear God saying to you. God has a prophetic message for you. Hear it now!

So I say, walk by the Spirit, and you will not gratify the desires of the flesh. Galatians 5:16

My spiritual insights and revelations:

Prayer No. 45

PROPHETIC PRAYER

*L*ord, thank you for opening my eyes to who you are. Thank you for enlightening me to know the importance of your glorious hope. Never let my eyes be closed again. Let me forever know the revelation of the truth and knowledge of who you are in my life.

I pray that the eyes of your heart may be enlightened in order that you may know the hope to which he has called you, the riches of his glorious inheritance in his holy people. Ephesians 1:18

My prayer for today:

Personal Reflections

There really is a spiritual battle going on around you that shows up in physical events. But don't be fooled. The real enemy is Satan. To defeat Satan, you need spiritual weaponry that comes from God. Access yours today.

For though we live in the world, we do not wage war as the world does. The weapons we fight with are not the weapons of the world. On the contrary, they have divine power to demolish strongholds. 2 Corinthians 10:3-4

My prayers, hopes, and dreams:

SPIRITUAL REVELATION

Let the following scripture speak to your heart as you meditate on it. Then, write down the things you hear God saying to you. God has a prophetic message for you. Hear it now!

> *The Spirit you received does not make you slaves, so that you live in fear again; rather, the Spirit you received brought about your adoption to sonship. And by him we cry, "Abba, Father."*
> *Romans 8:15*

My spiritual insights and revelations:

Prayer No. 46

PROPHETIC PRAYER

*J*ehovah God, I love that you are with me day and night. You are always present. I am grateful that I will always have cause for singing and praising you because of your loving kindness. Thank you for your love!

By day the Lord directs his love, at night his song is with me— a prayer to the God of my life. Psalm 42:8

My prayer for today:

PERSONAL REFLECTIONS

You are one of God's agents in the earth. He wants to use you to carry out his plan for mankind. You are backed by the prayers of the saints before you. Now go forward and be victorious!

> *In all my prayers for all of you, I always pray with joy because of your partnership in the gospel from the first day until now, being confident of this, that he who began a good work in you will carry it on to completion until the day of Christ Jesus. Philippians 1:4-6*

My prayers, hopes, and dreams:

SPIRITUAL REVELATION

Let the following scripture speak to your heart as you meditate on it. Then, write down the things you hear God saying to you. God has a prophetic message for you. Hear it now!

Never be lacking in zeal, but keep your spiritual fervor, serving the Lord. Romans 12:11

My spiritual insights and revelations:

Prayer No. 47

PROPHETIC PRAYER

Wise and Holy God, it is you who examines me. May you find me as righteous. Your eyes are the ones watching over me in the world. You keep me through the faults and failures of life. Thank you for providing me with your protection. I feel safe because of it.

For the eyes of the Lord are on the righteous and his ears are attentive to their prayer, but the face of the Lord is against those who do evil. 1 Peter 3:12

My prayer for today:

PERSONAL REFLECTIONS

Healing is possible through those who believe. Yes, it is a miracle, but it is one that you and others can experience through the prayers of believers in Christ Jesus. Ask a believer to intercede on your behalf. Prayer works!

> *Is anyone among you sick? Let them call the elders of the church to pray over them and anoint them with oil in the name of the Lord. And the prayer offered in faith will make the sick person well; the Lord will raise them up. If they have sinned, they will be forgiven. James 5:14-15*

My prayers, hopes, and dreams:

SPIRITUAL REVELATION

Let the following scripture speak to your heart as you meditate on it. Then, write down the things you hear God saying to you. God has a prophetic message for you. Hear it now!

The Spirit of the Sovereign Lord is on me, because the Lord has anointed me to proclaim good news to the poor. He has sent me to bind up the brokenhearted, to proclaim freedom for the captives and release from darkness for the prisoners. Isaiah 61:1

My spiritual insights and revelations:

Prayer No. 48

PROPHETIC PRAYER

*L*ord of all, I thank you for revealing your truth to me. Help me to keep watch and remain ready to meet you as life progresses. Help me not to be weighed down with the frustrations and issues of life's many circumstances. Keep me strong. I need you now and forever more.

The end of all things is near. Therefore be alert and of sober mind so that you may pray. 1 Peter 4:7

My prayer for today:

PERSONAL REFLECTIONS

There is only so much of a load that you can carry. You could be over your limit right now. Give it over to Jesus. Admitting that you need Jesus is not a weakness; it's wisdom.

> *Humble yourselves, therefore, under God's mighty hand, that he may lift you up in due time. 7 Cast all your anxiety on him because he cares for you. 1 Peter 5:6*

My prayers, hopes, and dreams:

Spiritual Revelation

Let the following scripture speak to your heart as you meditate on it. Then, write down the things you hear God saying to you. God has a prophetic message for you. Hear it now!

Since we live by the Spirit, let us keep in step with the Spirit.
Galatians 5:25

My spiritual insights and revelations:

Prayer No. 49

PROPHETIC PRAYER

*A*lmighty God, as I make my request to you, I am confident in knowing that my prayers have been received. You have never failed to answer me. And I thank you for that.

The Lord has heard my cry for mercy; the Lord accepts my prayer. Psalm 6:9

My prayer for today:

PERSONAL REFLECTIONS

When you pray, God is listening to you each and every time. You must believe that he will answer you. Therefore, don't hesitate to seek him, no matter the issue. God has a plan for you, too, according to his will. Find it!

This is the confidence we have in approaching God: that if we ask anything according to his will, he hears us. And if we know that he hears us—we ask—we know that we have what we asked of him. 1 John 5:14-15

My prayers, hopes, and dreams:

SPIRITUAL REVELATION

Let the following scripture speak to your heart as you meditate on it. Then, write down the things you hear God saying to you. God has a prophetic message for you. Hear it now!

Dear friends, do not believe every spirit, but test the spirits to see whether they are from God, because many false prophets have gone out into the world.
1 John 4:1

My spiritual insights and revelations:

Prayer No. 50

PROPHETIC PRAYER

*L*ord God, I come before you sincerely with an open heart. I know that a righteous prayer will motivate you to listen. Accept the prayer of my heart and the words I pour out to you as my best effort to petition you.

Hear me, Lord, my plea is just; listen to my cry. Hear my prayer— it does not rise from deceitful lips. Psalm 17:1

My prayer for today:

PERSONAL REFLECTIONS

Life can be frightening sometimes. But you don't have to live in fear. This is not what God wants for you. So when you are intimidated, pray to God to settle your mind and spirit to feel his power moving inside of you. God will bring you through your most fearful moments.

For the Spirit God gave us does not make us timid, but gives us power, love and self-discipline.
2 Timothy 1:7

My prayers, hopes, and dreams:

SPIRITUAL REVELATION

Let the following scripture speak to your heart as you meditate on it. Then, write down the things you hear God saying to you. God has a prophetic message for you. Hear it now!

The mind governed by the flesh is death, but the mind governed by the Spirit is life and peace.
Romans 8:6

My spiritual insights and revelations:

Prayer No. 51

PROPHETIC PRAYER

*L*ord God, it has been my constant course to come to you for assistance and deliverance. I know you might delay for a season, but I am still confident that you are an on time God. I know you hear my prayer!

I call on you, my God, for you will answer me; turn your ear to me and hear my prayer. Psalm 17:6

My prayer for today:

PERSONAL REFLECTIONS

You cannot avoid all the troubles of life. In fact, you might suffer many troubling moments, even as a believer. But God is still in charge of life. He will deliver you from them all. Keep believing in him. God is on your side!

The righteous person may have many troubles, but the Lord delivers him from them all; he protects all his bones, not one of them will be broken. Psalm 34:19-20

My prayers, hopes, and dreams:

SPIRITUAL REVELATION

Let the following scripture speak to your heart as you meditate on it. Then, write down the things you hear God saying to you. God has a prophetic message for you. Hear it now!

God is spirit, and his worshipers must worship in the Spirit and in truth. John 4:24

My spiritual insights and revelations:

Prayer No. 52

PROPHETIC PRAYER

Gracious God, I express my thankfulness up to you every time I petition you in prayer. I acknowledge and honor the gift of grace because of whom I serve. It's through Jesus Christ that I have been renewed. Thank you!

I give thanks to my God always for you because of the grace of God that was given you in Christ Jesus. 1 Corinthians 1:4

My prayer for today:

PERSONAL REFLECTIONS

It can get hard to make it through life. The many obstacles can challenge you and your faith. But your strength comes from God. Expect his power to be the source of your power and deliverance. There is no force that can stand against God!

> *Finally, be strong in the Lord and in his mighty power. Put on the full armor of God, so that you can take your stand against the devil's schemes. For our struggle is not against flesh and blood, but against the rulers, against the authorities, against the powers of this dark world and against the spiritual forces of evil in the heavenly realms.*
> *Ephesians 6:10-12*

My prayers, hopes, and dreams:

Spiritual Revelation

Let the following scripture speak to your heart as you meditate on it. Then, write down the things you hear God saying to you. God has a prophetic message for you. Hear it now!

But the fruit of the Spirit is love, joy, peace, forbearance, kindness, goodness, faithfulness, gentleness and self-control. Against such things there is no law. Galatians 5:22-23

My spiritual insights and revelations:

Benediction Prayer

Now that you have prayed and heard God's desire for you, I want to pray a blessing over your life. But I want you to pray it with me aloud as your prayer. Let us pray:

Lord God, I thank you for the opportunity to petition you in prayer. May my prayer turn into worship and my worship show up as praise. Sovereign Lord, you made the heavens and the earth, the sea, and everything in them. You alone are God. Everything that exists came from you. You can handle my most challenging moments and you can calm my greatest fears.

Lord, I thank you for deliverance from the bondages of life. I thank you for helping me to overcome the struggles and hardships I've faced. You have been my salvation. You have been my protector. You are the Lord of my life.

Lord, I also thank you for joy in my life. I thank you for hope and peace. And Lord, I thank you for the love that sustains me. You are my Lord. I adore you.

Lord, I give you praise, glory, and honor for who you are in my life. You are my God. I pray this in the name of Jesus Christ, Amen.

God heard you when you prayed! Stand on that as your confession of faith. Accept the blessings from God as they continue to flow into your life. Continue to pray as God continues to bless you.

To him who is able to keep you from stumbling and to present you before his glorious presence without fault and with great joy—to the only God our Savior be glory, majesty, power and authority, through Jesus Christ our Lord, before all ages, now and forevermore! Amen. Jude 1:24-25

Printed in the United States
By Bookmasters